Series Editor: Pie Corbett

CAMBRIDGE UNIVERSITY PRESS
Cambridge, New York, Melbourne, Madrid, Cape Town, Singapore, São Paulo

Cambridge University Press
The Edinburgh Building, Cambridge CB2 2RU, UK

www.cambridge.org
Information on this title: www.cambridge.org/9780521618908

First published 2006

Printed in the United Kingdom at the University Press, Cambridge

A catalogue record for this publication is available from the British Library

ISBN-13   978-0-521-61890-8 paperback
ISBN-10   0-521-61890-8 paperback

ACKNOWLEDGEMENTS

Cover
Illustration (Bill Greenhead)

Artwork
Beehive Illustration (Russell Becker, Pulsar, Peter Richardson), Illustration (Paul Daviz, Nick Diggory, John Paul Early, Bill Greenhead).

Texts
'Benediction' from *Chain of Days* by James Berry (© James Berry, 1985) is reproduced by permission of PFD (www.pfd.co.uk) on behalf of James Berry; 'Jabberwocky' by Lewis Carroll; 'In the Time of the Wolf' by Gillian Clarke from *The Animal Wall* published by Pont Books; 'We Are Not Alone' by Paul Cookson; 'Howl' © Jan Dean from *Wallpapering the Cat* published by Macmillan 2003; 'Who's There?' © Jan Dean from *A Mean Fish Smile* by Roger Stevens, Sue Cowling & Jan Dean – Macmillan 2000; 'Pheasant' and 'Island Dinosaur' by Gina Douthwaite, published by Red Fox. Reprinted by permission of The Random House Group Ltd.; 'Didgeridoo' by Roger McGough from *Bad, Bad Cats* (© Roger McGough 1997) is reproduced by permission of PFD (www.pfd.co.uk) on behalf of Roger McGough; 'The Highwayman' by Alfred Noyes. Permission granted by The Society of Authors as the Literary Representative of the Estate of Alfred Noyes; 'The Magical Mouse' by Kenneth Patchen, from *The Collected Poems of Kenneth Patchen*, copyright © 1957 by New Directions Publishing Corp. Reprinted by permission of New Directions Publishing Corp.; 'Tiger Shadows' © Brian Patten 2000 / 1990 / 1985. Reproduced by permission of the author c/o Rogers, Coleridge & White Ltd., 20 Powis Mews, London W11 1JN; 'Dazzledance' by John Rice from *The Dream of Night Fishers*, Scottish Cultural Press, 1998.

Contents

Significant poets

Dragonbirth

In the midnight mists
of long ago
On a far-off mountainside
there stood
a wild oak wood...

In the wild, wet wood
there grew an oak;
beneath the oak
there slept a cave
and in that cave
the mosses crept.
Beneath the moss
there lay a stone,
beneath the stone
there lay an egg,
and in that egg
there was a crack.
From that crack
there breathed a flame;
from that flame
there burst a fire,
and from that fire

dragon came.

Judith Nicholls

Dragon Night

A dragon creeps
into my head
and wanders,
stealthy as a moon,
when day is left behind.
At dead of night,
as light as air,
as dark as lead
she sneaks,
in silence;
creeps into my head,
into my mind.

A dragon prowls
into my mind
and presses,
silent as a star,
into my dreams.
When day is left behind,
on padded feet
she treads through darkness,

pressing, pressing,
silently she presses
through the forests
of my mind.

A dragon roars
into the night,
hurls flames,
as fiery as a sun,
before my eyes, behind;
scours shadows into life
and thunders, panting
fire that sets alight
the forests of my dreams.
The dragon roars
into my night,
into my mind.

Judith Nicholls

Green Man, Blue Man

As I was walking through Guildhall Square
I smiled to see a green man there,
But when I saw him coming near
My heart was filled with nameless fear.

As I was walking through Madford Lane
A blue man stood there in the rain.
I asked him in my front-door,
For I'd seen a blue man before.

As I was walking through Landlake Wood
A grey man in the forest stood,
But when he turned and said, "Good day"
I shook my head and ran away.

As I was walking by Church Stile
A purple man spoke there a while.
I spoke to him because, you see,
A purple man once lived by me.

But when the night falls dark and fell
How, O how, am I to tell,
Grey man, green man, purple, blue,
Which is which is which of you?

Charles Causley

My Mother Saw a Dancing Bear

My mother saw a dancing bear

By the schoolyard, a day in June.

The keeper stood with chain and bar

And whistle-pipe, and played a tune.

And bruin lifted up its head
And lifted up its dusty feet,
And all the children laughed to see
It caper in the summer heat.

They watched as for the Queen it died.
They watched it march. They watched it halt.
They heard the keeper as he cried,
"Now, roly-poly!" "Somersault!"

And then, my mother said, there came
The keeper with a begging-cup,
The bear with burning coat of fur,
Shaming the laughter to a stop.

They paid a penny for the dance,
But what they saw was not the show;
Only, in bruin's aching eyes,
Far-distant forests, and the snow.

Charles Causley

Pheasant

Pheasant strutting
like a lord
in green-sheen balaclava,
trying to attract a mate
so he can be a father,
flicks his tick of
yellow eye,

hides pride behind a mask, displays his vicar's collar in this mixed-up-
matching task. He preens red pencilled feathers, shakes shavings from his
back and points a scaly leg as though he's ready to attack the dull brown
bird he's spotted but greets her with a cry that's like a throttled
engine that's threatening to die.

She turns
away, this dull
brown bird, plays
hard-to-get which
brings a ruffle to
his plumage, a
clockwork whir of
wings, a launching
of his body, a
tearing of his
mind – divided as
his airborne tail
as he leaves her
behind.

Gina Douthwaite

Island Dinosaur

I see
an island in
the sea. It's like   a dinosaur. Its
    sleepy eye   of sun awakes as I
        watch from the shore. Its rocky back is
          rough and black upon its bed of waves. It
            yawns a hungry warning to the fishes in its
              caves, then lumbers up on lumpy legs –
                its frilly socks start slipping round its ankles
                  as it wades, stumbling and tripping, from the sea
                bed where   it's slept a   million years
              or more. And   only I have   seen it
              wake – my   island dino-   saur.

Gina Douthwaite

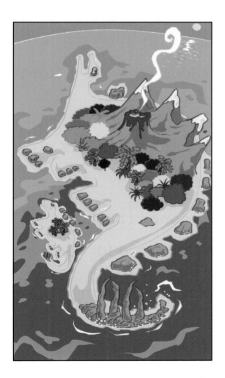

Tiger Shadows

I wish I was a tiger in the Indian jungle

The jungle would be my teacher

No school

And the night sky a blackboard smudged with stars

I wish I was a tiger in the Indian jungle

Kitten-curious

I'd pad about on paws big as frying pans

While the monkeys chatted in the trees above me

I'd sniff the damp jungly air

Out of exotic flowers I would make a crown of pollen

If I were a tiger in the Indian jungle

My eyes would glitter among the dark green leaves

My tail would twitch like a snake

I would discover abandoned cities

Where no human feet had trod for centuries

I would be lord of a lost civilization

And leap among the vine-covered ruins

I wish I was a tiger in the Indian jungle

As the evening fell

I'd hum quiet tiger-tunes to
    which the fireflies would
    dance

I'd watch the red,
    bubbling sun
Go fishing with its net
    of shadows

While the hunters
    looked for me miles
    and miles away
I'd lie stretched out in
    my secret den

I would doze in the
    strawberry-coloured
    light

Under the golden stripy
    shadows of the trees
I would dream a tiger's dream

Brian Patten

Didgeridoo

Catfish

take catnaps on seabeds

Sticklebacks

stick like glue

Terrapins

are terrific with needles

But what does a didgery do?

Bloodhounds

play good rounds of poker

Chihuahuas

do nothing but chew

Poodles

make puddles to paddle in

But what does a didgery do?

A puffin

will stuff in a muffin

A canary

can nearly canoe

Humming-birds

hum something rotten

But what does a didgery do?

Tapeworms

play tapes while out jogging

Flies

feed for free at the zoo

Headlice

use headlights at night-time

But what does a didgery do?

What does a didgery

What does a didgery

What does a didgeridoo?

Roger McGough

The Magical Mouse

I am the magical mouse

I don't eat cheese

I eat sunsets

And the tops of trees

I don't wear fur

I wear funnels

Of lost ships and the weather

That's under dead leaves

I am the magical mouse

I don't fear cats

Or woodsowls

I do as I please

Always

I don't eat crusts

I am the magical mouse

I eat

Little birds – and maidens

That taste like dust

Kenneth Patchen

Longer classic and narrative poetry

The Highwayman

The wind was a torrent of darkness among the gusty trees,
The moon was a ghostly galleon tossed upon cloudy seas.
The road was a ribbon of moonlight over the purple moor,
And the highwayman came riding –
    Riding – riding –
The highwayman came riding, up to the old inn-door.

He'd a French cocked-hat on his forehead, a bunch of lace at
        his chin,
A coat of the claret velvet, and breeches of brown doe-skin.
They fitted with never a wrinkle. His boots were up to the thigh.
And he rode with a jewelled twinkle,
    His pistol butts a-twinkle,
His rapier hilt a-twinkle, under the jewelled sky.

Over the cobbles he clattered and clashed in the dark inn-yard.
He tapped with his whip on the shutters, but all was locked
        and barred.
He whistled a tune to the window, and who should be waiting there
But the landlord's black-eyed daughter,
    Bess, the landlord's daughter,
Plaiting a dark red love-knot into her long black hair.

And dark in the dark old inn-yard a stable-wicket creaked
Where Tim the ostler listened. His face was white and peaked.

His eyes were hollows of madness, his hair like mouldy hay,
But he loved the landlord's daughter,
    The landlord's red-lipped daughter.
Dumb as a dog he listened, and he heard the robber say –

"One kiss, my bonny sweetheart, I'm after a prize tonight,
But I shall be back with the yellow gold before the morning light;
Yet, if they press me sharply, and harry me through the day,
Then look for me by moonlight,
    Watch for me by moonlight,
I'll come to thee by moonlight, though hell should bar the way."

He rose upright in the stirrups. He scarce could reach her hand,
But she loosened her hair i' the casement. His face burnt like
        a brand
As the black cascade of perfume came tumbling over his breast;
And he kissed its waves in the moonlight,
    (Oh, sweet black waves in the moonlight!)
Then he tugged at his rein in the moonlight, and galloped away
        to the west.

He did not come in the
    dawning. He did not
    come at noon;
And out o' the tawny sunset,
    before the rise o' the
    moon,
When the road was a gypsy's
    ribbon, looping the
    purple moor,
A red-coat troop came
    marching –
    Marching – marching –
King George's men came
    marching, up to the old
    inn-door.

They said no word to the
    landlord. They drank his ale instead.
But they gagged his daughter, and bound her, to the foot of her
    narrow bed.
Two of them knelt at her casement, with muskets at their side!
There was death at every window;
    And hell at one dark window;
For Bess could see, through her casement, the road that he
    would ride.

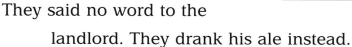

They had tied her up to attention, with many a sniggering jest.

They had bound a musket beside her, with the muzzle beneath
      her breast!

"Now, keep good watch!" and they kissed her.
    She heard the dead man say –

Look for me by moonlight;
    Watch for me by moonlight;

I'll come to thee by moonlight, though hell should bar the way!

She twisted her hands behind her; but all the knots held good!

She writhed her hands till her fingers were wet with sweat
      or blood!

They stretched and strained in the darkness, and the hours
      crawled by like years,

Till, now, on the stroke of midnight,
    Cold, on the stroke of midnight,

The tip of one finger touched it! The trigger at least was hers!

The tip of one finger touched it. She strove no more for the rest.

Up, she stood up to attention, with the muzzle beneath her breast.

She would not risk their hearing; she would not strive again;

For the road lay bare in the moonlight;
    Blank and bare in the moonlight;

And the blood of her veins, in the moonlight, throbbed to her
      love's refrain.

Tlot-tlot; tlot-tlot! Had they
> heard it? The horse-
> hoofs ringing clear;
Tlot-tlot; tlot-tlot, in the
> distance! Were they
> deaf that they did
> not hear?
Down the ribbon of
> moonlight, over the
> brow of the hill,
The highwayman came
> riding,
> > Riding, riding!
The red-coats looked to their
> priming! She stood up,
> straight and still.

Tlot-tlot, in the frosty silence!
> Tlot-tlot, in the echoing night!
Nearer he came and nearer.
> Her face was like a light.
Her eyes grew wide for a moment; she drew one last deep breath,
Then her finger moved in the moonlight,
> Her musket shattered the moonlight,
Shattered her breast in the moonlight and warned him – with
> her death.

He turned. He spurred to the west; he did not know who stood
Bowed, with her head o'er the musket, drenched with her
     own red blood!
Not till the dawn he heard it, and his face grew grey to hear
How Bess, the landlord's daughter,
   The landlord's black-eyed daughter,
Had watched for her love in the moonlight, and died in the
     darkness there.

Back, he spurred like a madman, shouting a curse to the sky,
With the white road smoking behind him and his rapier
     brandished high.
Blood-red were his spurs i' the golden noon; wine-red was his
     velvet coat;
When they shot him down on the highway,
   Down like a dog on the highway,
And he lay in his blood on the highway, with the bunch of lace
     at his throat.

And still of a winter's night, they say, when the wind is in the trees,
When the moon is a ghostly galleon tossed upon cloudy seas,
When the road is a ribbon of moonlight over the purple moor,
A highwayman comes riding –
   Riding – riding –
A highwayman comes riding, up to the old inn-door.

Over the cobbles he clatters and clangs in the dark inn-yard.

And he taps with his whip on the shutters, but all is locked and
barred.

He whistles a tune to the window, and who should be waiting
there

But the landlord's black-eyed daughter,

Bess, the landlord's daughter,

Plaiting a dark red love-knot into her long black hair.

Alfred Noyes

Performance poetry

We Are Not Alone

When the floorboards creak and the hinges squeak

The TV's off but seems to speak

When the moon is full and you hear a shriek

We are not alone.

When the spiders gather beneath your bed

When they colonise the garden shed

When they spin their webs right above your head

We are not alone.

When the lights are out and there's no-one home

You're by yourself and you're on your own

The radiators bubble and groan

We are not alone.

When the shadows lengthen round your wall

You hear deep breathing in the hall

You think there's no-one there at all

We are not alone.

When the branches tap on your window pane

The finger twigs scritch scratch again

When something's changed but it looks the same

We are not alone.

When the wallpaper is full of eyes

The toys in the dark all change in size

Anything's a monster in disguise

We are not alone.

You'd better watch out whatever you do

There's something out there looking at you

When you think you're on your own

We are not

We are not

We are not alone.

Paul Cookson

Who's There?

Nobody breaks the windows,

Nobody spills the milk.

Nobody creeps round the house at night

As silent and secret as smooth black silk.

Nobody digs deep holes in the garden,

Nobody scratches long scars in the wall.

I am afraid of Nobody.

When I'm alone will Nobody call?

Nobody whispers scary stories

To frighten the little ones tucked in their beds.

Nobody growls and makes wicked noises

To make them pull covers over their heads.

When there's just me by myself, I will shudder.

Hush myself. Still myself. Shiver with fear,

Because, in the shadows, I know who is waiting –

Watchful and hungry – Nobody's here…

Jan Dean

Jabberwocky

'Twas brillig, and the slithy toves
Did gyre and gimble in the wabe;
All mimsy were the borogoves,
And the mome raths outgrabe.

"Beware the Jabberwock, my son!
The jaws that bite, the claws that catch!
Beware the Jubjub bird, and shun
The frumious Bandersnatch!"

He took his vorpal sword in hand:
Long time the manxome foe he sought –
So rested he by the Tumtum tree,
And stood awhile in thought.

And as in uffish thought he stood,
The Jabberwock, with eyes of flame,
Came whiffling through the tulgey wood,
And burbled as it came!

One, two! One, two! And through and through

The vorpal blade went snicker-snack!

He left it dead, and with its head

He went galumphing back.

"And hast thou slain the Jabberwock?

Come to my arms, my beamish boy!

O frabjous day! Callooh! Callay!"

He chortled in his joy.

'Twas brillig, and the slithy toves

Did gyre and gimble in the wabe;

All mimsy were the borogoves,

And the mome raths outgrabe.

Lewis Carroll

Howl

Ride the wolf and see the forest
Flick and fly beside your eye –
See the white frost gleam and glitter
As the winter wolf speeds by.

Ride the wolf – thread your fine fingers
Through the grey hair of his mane.
Touch the roughness, feel the chaffing,
Wonder – will we come again
　　　To the soft time, to the safe time,
　　　To the time of stout stone walls,
　　　To the tame time of the fireside,
　　　To the story-tellers halls?

Ride the wolf and let the moonlight
Sink like silver in your skin.
Breathe the ice blades of the fierce air,
Cut your ties with human kin.
Let the wilderness outside you
Join the wilderness within…

The frozen stars will shatter at the shiver of his howl.

No shadow is as subtle or as secret as his prowl.

The grey lord of the winter will not be denied,

So step out of the firelight and

Ride! Ride! Ride!

Jan Dean

In the Time of the Wolf

Who sings the legend?
The mouse in the rafters,
the owl in the forest,
the wind in the mountains,
the tumbling river.

Where can we read it?
In a shadow on the grass,
in the footprint in the sand,
in reflections on the water,
in the fossil in the stone.

How shall we keep it?
In the lake of history,
in the box called memory,
in the voice of the teller,
in the ear of the child.

How will we tell it?

With a tongue of lightning,

with a drum of thunder,

with a strumming of grasses,

with a whisper of wind.

Gillian Clarke

Dazzledance

I have an eye of silver,
I have an eye of gold,
I have a tongue of reed-grass
   and a story to be told.

I have a hand of metal,
I have a hand of clay,
I have two arms of granite
   and a song for every day.

I have a foot of damson,
I have a foot of corn,
I have two legs of leaf-stalk
   and a dance for every morn.

I have a dream of water,
I have a dream of snow,
I have a thought of wildfire
   and a harp-string long and low.

I have an eye of silver,
I have an eye of gold,
I have a tongue of reed-grass
   and a story to be told.

John Rice

Benediction

Thanks to the ear
that someone may hear

Thanks to seeing
that someone may see

Thanks to feeling
that someone may feel

Thanks to touch
that one may be touched

Thanks to flowering of white moon
and spreading shawl of black night
holding villages and cities together

James Berry